Welcome to **Winter Tales: Holiday Legacy Challenges for The Sims 4**, a celebration of festive storytelling and creative gameplay designed to bring the holiday season to life in your Sims' worlds. Whether you're an experienced player or just starting out, this collection is here to spark your imagination and fill your game with warmth, joy, and a touch of holiday magic.

The holidays are all about stories—of connection, resilience, and traditions that bring us together. This book invites you to explore those themes through unique gameplay challenges that guide your Sims on adventures full of creativity and heart. From building communities to crafting magical moments, each challenge offers an opportunity to create your own unforgettable *Winter Tales*.

Whether you love starting from scratch, embracing a bit of magic, or weaving generational stories, this book has something to inspire you. These challenges are designed to fit a variety of playstyles, encouraging you to blend the magic of the season with the unique quirks of your Sims. Together, they'll transform your gameplay into a cozy holiday experience filled with surprises.

Thank you for joining me on this journey into the holiday spirit. I hope these tales inspire you to create your own, filled with laughter, wonder, and plenty of festive cheer.

Happy holidays, and happy Simming!
—Emma

Rekindling Yule:
A Post-Apocalyptic Holiday Challenge

The year was 2040, and the world was preparing for its grandest Christmas celebration yet. Cities sparkled with holiday lights, snow fell gently on rooftops, and carollers filled the air with cheer. But in a cruel twist of fate, the joy of the season turned to chaos when the *Great Christmas Catastrophe* struck.

No one knows exactly how it began. Was it a botched experiment with holiday magic? An energy overload from all the lights and decorations? Or perhaps, an ancient curse unleashed by the greed of the season? All that remains are whispers of a Christmas storm so fierce it tore apart the skies, blanketed the world in unending frost, and plunged society into darkness. The joy of the holidays was lost, replaced by fear and survival.

Years later, amid the ruins of civilization, a brave soul emerges in Newcrest, a barren and forgotten land. Fuelled by hope and the memories of a brighter time, you vow to rebuild—not just a town, but the very spirit of Christmas. You'll face the harsh realities of a world left in ruin, scavenging for supplies and fighting to survive, but through it all, you'll nurture a spark of holiday magic to light the way forward.

Each generation of your family will take on a new challenge, building homes, farms, businesses, and community spaces to restore Newcrest to its former glory. Together, they will create a town filled with holiday cheer, proving that even after the darkest nights, Christmas can shine brightly again.

The future of the holidays is in your hands. Will you rise to the challenge and rebuild a world where Christmas joy reigns supreme?

Generation 1: The Christmas Survivor

Story Challenge:
The Great Christmas Catastrophe has left the world in ruins. You're one of the few survivors, determined to rebuild a new life. Armed with only a survival kit and the memory of holiday cheer, you set out to lay the foundations of a new Christmas legacy.

- **Aspiration:** Extreme Sports Enthusiast
- **Personality Traits:** Ambitious, Loves Outdoors, Brave
- **Lot Traits:** Off the Grid, Simple Living
- **Lot Challenges:** Creepy Crawlies, Filthy

Bucket List:

1. Start with zero simoleons and build a survival shelter using earned funds.
2. Max the Gardening skill to grow food and create a holiday tree farm.
3. Craft survival items using the Fabrication and Handiness skills.
4. Host a rudimentary Winterfest celebration with handmade decorations.
5. Create a Christmas survival guide to pass down to the next generation.

Area to Build:
A survival shelter with a basic garden and small holiday-themed touches (e.g., a handcrafted wreath or tree).

Generation 2: The Holiday Scavenger

Story Challenge:
Resources are scarce, but you're resourceful. You scour the wasteland to find materials to expand your family's shelter and bring some semblance of Christmas magic back to life.

- **Aspiration:** Curator
- **Personality Traits:** Creative, Cheerful, Self-Assured
- **Lot Traits:** Homey, Great Soil
- **Lot Challenges:** Reduce and Recycle, Wild Foxes

Bucket List:

1. Collect rare items, including holiday-themed relics, and display them in your home.
2. Max the Fabrication skill and craft holiday furniture.
3. Host a scavenger Winterfest party, where gifts are made from scavenged materials.
4. Build a small workshop to craft and repair items for the community.
5. Pass down a family heirloom scavenged from the wasteland.

Area to Build:
An expanded shelter with a workshop and displays of scavenged holiday treasures.

Generation 3: The Christmas Cultivator

Story Challenge:
Food supplies are dwindling, but you see an opportunity to create sustainable living for your family and neighbors. Your dream is to establish a holiday-themed farm that provides for everyone while spreading hope.

- **Aspiration:** Freelance Botanist
- **Personality Traits:** Loves Outdoors, Good, Cheerful
- **Lot Traits:** Great Soil, Natural Well
- **Lot Challenges:** Simple Living, Filthy

Bucket List:

1. Grow perfect-quality crops and create a thriving garden.
2. Breed animals (e.g., chickens, cows) to create a sustainable food source.
3. Build a greenhouse to grow winter plants and holiday trees.
4. Host a community Winterfest feast using homegrown ingredients.
5. Pass down a family recipe inspired by your garden.

Area to Build:
A farmstead with a greenhouse, crops, and animals, all decorated for the holidays.

Generation 4: The Festive Engineer

Story Challenge:
The infrastructure is crumbling, but you dream of creating a new power grid infused with the magic of Christmas. Your goal is to use your engineering skills to bring light and power back to Newcrest.

- **Aspiration:** Nerd Brain
- **Personality Traits:** Genius, Perfectionist, Cheerful
- **Lot Traits:** Science Lair, Convivial
- **Lot Challenges:** Gremlins, Reduce and Recycle

Bucket List:

1. Max the Handiness and Logic skills.
2. Build a fully functional power grid to light up your home and community.
3. Create holiday-themed electronics or decorations (e.g., a light display).
4. Host a "Lighting of the Tree" Winterfest ceremony.
5. Pass down a handcrafted invention to the next generation.

Area to Build:
A workshop and utility station with a dazzling holiday light display.

Generation 5: The Christmas Defender

Story Challenge:
The wasteland is still dangerous, and it's up to you to protect your family and community. As a skilled fighter, you train others to defend themselves while fostering holiday hope.

- **Aspiration:** Bodybuilder
- **Personality Traits:** Brave, Active, Family-Oriented
- **Lot Traits:** Private Dwelling, Peace and Quiet
- **Lot Challenges:** Creepy Crawlies, Grody

Bucket List:

1. Max the Fitness and Handiness skills.
2. Build a training center for self-defense classes.
3. Host a Winterfest gathering where you honor fallen survivors.
4. Befriend and protect five Sims in need.
5. Pass down a survival weapon or artifact as a family heirloom.

Area to Build:
A training center and community safe zone with festive holiday elements.

Generation 6: The Holiday Trader

Story Challenge:
Trade has begun to flourish, and you aim to bring the spirit of giving to the marketplace. Your dream is to establish a bustling holiday market in Newcrest.

- **Aspiration:** Fabulously Wealthy
- **Personality Traits:** Outgoing, Cheerful, Ambitious
- **Lot Traits:** Homey, Great Acoustics
- **Lot Challenges:** Reduce and Recycle, Filthy

Bucket List:

1. Max the Charisma and Entrepreneur skills.
2. Build a market plaza with stalls selling holiday-themed items.
3. Host a Winterfest market event with games, music, and gifts.
4. Trade with five Sims to bring unique goods to the market.
5. Pass down a family business tradition or skill.

Area to Build:
A holiday-themed market plaza with vibrant stalls and festive décor.

Generation 7: The Jolly Architect

Story Challenge:

The town needs homes and shelters, and you've taken it upon yourself to rebuild Newcrest as a festive haven. Your mission is to create beautiful, holiday-inspired homes for future generations.

- **Aspiration:** Mansion Baron
- **Personality Traits:** Creative, Perfectionist, Ambitious
- **Lot Traits:** Home Studio, Natural Light
- **Lot Challenges:** Gremlins, Cursed

Bucket List:

1. Max the Handiness and Painting skills.
2. Build and decorate at least three holiday-themed homes for Sims.
3. Host a "Home for the Holidays" event, inviting Sims to see your creations.
4. Design a unique holiday room for your family's home.
5. Pass down a blueprint for a family home.

Area to Build:

A row of festive homes that bring life back to Newcrest.

Generation 8: The Christmas Visionary

Story Challenge:
You dream of restoring Newcrest's culture and sense of community by creating a holiday arts center. Your goal is to use creativity to inspire hope and unity.

- **Aspiration:** Painter Extraordinaire
- **Personality Traits:** Creative, Outgoing, Cheerful
- **Lot Traits:** Convivial, Great Acoustics
- **Lot Challenges:** Grody, Reduce and Recycle

Bucket List:

1. Max the Painting and Photography skills.
2. Build a festive arts center for the community.
3. Host a holiday art show featuring your work.
4. Teach at least three Sims how to create holiday crafts.
5. Pass down a family art collection or gallery.

Area to Build:
An arts center with festive décor, galleries, and craft rooms.

Generation 9: The Holiday Healer

Story Challenge:
The population is growing, but so are health challenges. Your dream is to build a clinic that helps Sims thrive during the holidays and beyond.

- **Aspiration:** Friend of the World
- **Personality Traits:** Good, Cheerful, Ambitious
- **Lot Traits:** Peace and Quiet, Great Acoustics
- **Lot Challenges:** Simple Living, Filthy

Bucket List:

1. Max the Wellness and Parenting skills.
2. Build a holiday-themed clinic or wellness spa.
3. Provide free healthcare or wellness services during Winterfest.
4. Host a "Holiday Healing" event to bring the community together.
5. Pass down a healing tradition or practice.

Area to Build:
A wellness center or clinic with festive, calming holiday touches.

Generation 10: The Christmas Savior

Story Challenge:

As the final generation, your mission is to transform Newcrest into a thriving, festive town where the Christmas spirit shines bright. Build the ultimate Winterfest plaza to unite all Sims in joy.

- **Aspiration:** Party Animal
- **Personality Traits:** Outgoing, Cheerful, Creative
- **Lot Traits:** Festive Aura, Convivial
- **Lot Challenges:** Gremlins, Cursed

Bucket List:

1. Build a grand Winterfest plaza with lights, trees, and holiday markets.
2. Host a gold-level Winterfest festival for the entire community.
3. Complete a family time capsule with heirlooms from every generation.
4. Max the Charisma and Event Planning skills.
5. Pass down the ultimate family holiday tradition.

Area to Build:

A festive town square with dazzling lights, markets, and community gathering spaces.

The Christmas Chronicles:
A Decades Legacy

In the early 1900s, a young family fled the struggles of their homeland, settling in the empty, snow-blanketed expanse of Newcrest. Their hearts burned with a dream to build a legacy rooted in hope, resilience, and the magic of Christmas. With nothing but a few tools and their determination, they began their journey to create a home filled with warmth and joy.

Each generation carries the torch, adapting to the trials and triumphs of their time. From the rustic simplicity of the early 20th century to the roaring parties of the Jazz Age, the hardship of the Great Depression, and the unity forged during wartime, every chapter of their story reflects the changing face of Christmas.

As the decades pass, traditions evolve, but the family's mission remains steadfast: to spread love, laughter, and light during the darkest times. They build markets and theaters, create music and art, and even embrace modern technology, weaving the fabric of a holiday-inspired town that celebrates both history and innovation.

By the end of the century, Newcrest shines as a living testament to their dreams. From humble beginnings, the family transforms an empty land into a vibrant community where Christmas magic thrives year-round, honoring the past while inspiring the future. Will you guide them through the decades and ensure their holiday legacy lives on?

Generation 1: 1900s – The Christmas Pioneer

Story Challenge:
In this era, Christmas is simple and rooted in tradition. You've moved to a new land with little to your name. Your family starts with nothing but a dream of building a holiday legacy. Without modern conveniences, you must rely on hard work and resourcefulness.

- **Lot Traits:** Off the Grid, Simple Living
- **Aspiration:** Freelance Botanist
- **Personality Traits:** Ambitious, Family-Oriented, Loves Outdoors
- **Likes/Dislikes:** Likes gardening, fishing, and rustic furniture. Dislikes modern appliances.

Bucket List:

1. Build a home from scratch with only essential items.
2. Max the Gardening skill and grow a holiday tree.
3. Cook all meals using ingredients you've grown or foraged.
4. Celebrate Winterfest with handmade decorations only.
5. Befriend Father Winter and invite him to your Winterfest meal.

Generation 2: 1910s – The Merry Merchant

Story Challenge:
As cities grow, your family sees opportunity in the bustling holiday markets. You dream of becoming a merchant, selling handcrafted goods and seasonal treats. Your home is modest but cozy, filled with handmade crafts.

- **Lot Traits:** Homey, Great Acoustics
- **Aspiration:** Master Maker
- **Personality Traits:** Creative, Cheerful, Self-Assured
- **Likes/Dislikes:** Likes crafting, festive décor, and live music. Dislikes laziness.

Bucket List:

1. Sell at least 15 holiday-themed items on Plopsy.
2. Max the Fabrication and Baking skills.
3. Create a home shop or market stall to sell goods.
4. Build a collection of festive handcrafted decorations.
5. Host a community Winterfest party in your home.

Generation 3: 1920s – The Jazz Age Cheerleader

Story Challenge:

The roaring 20s bring jazz, flappers, and a love of excess. You embody the festive spirit of the decade, hosting glamorous Winterfest parties with music, dancing, and laughter. Your goal is to bring joy to everyone you meet.

- **Lot Traits:** Party Place, Great Acoustics
- **Aspiration:** Party Animal
- **Personality Traits:** Outgoing, Self-Assured, Music Lover
- **Likes/Dislikes:** Likes dancing, music, and vibrant colors. Dislikes quiet.

Bucket List:

1. Host at least three gold-level holiday parties.
2. Max the Dancing and Charisma skills.
3. Perform holiday songs on an instrument in public venues.
4. Woohoo under a mistletoe at a Winterfest party.
5. Befriend at least 20 Sims and invite them to your parties.

Generation 4: 1930s – The Christmas Provider

Story Challenge:

During the Great Depression, times are tough, but you still manage to find joy in simple holiday traditions. Your goal is to ensure your family has everything they need and that no Sim goes hungry during the holidays.

- **Lot Traits:** Grody, Simple Living
- **Aspiration:** Successful Lineage
- **Personality Traits:** Gloomy, Good, Family-Oriented
- **Likes/Dislikes:** Likes baking, cooking, and giving back. Dislikes wastefulness.

Bucket List:

1. Max the Cooking and Gourmet Cooking skills.
2. Volunteer with your family during Winterfest.
3. Host a simple but heartfelt Winterfest dinner with homemade meals.
4. Grow and harvest all ingredients for your holiday meals.
5. Gift handmade or foraged items to at least 5 Sims.

Generation 5: 1940s – The Festive Soldier

Story Challenge:
With the world at war, you've dedicated your life to protecting others. Despite hardship, you never lose your holiday spirit, spreading cheer to your community and keeping hope alive.

- **Lot Traits:** Peace and Quiet, Private Dwelling
- **Aspiration:** Neighborhood Confidante
- **Personality Traits:** Brave, Good, Active
- **Likes/Dislikes:** Likes fitness, family gatherings, and patriotic themes. Dislikes negativity.

Bucket List:

1. Reach level 5 in the Military career (if available) or Fitness skill.
2. Befriend at least 10 Sims and help them with errands or tasks.
3. Host a community potluck Winterfest dinner.
4. Collect and display war-era memorabilia.
5. Create a scrapbook documenting your holiday traditions.

Generation 6: 1950s – The Christmas Homemaker

Story Challenge:

The post-war boom ushers in a new era of domestic bliss. You take pride in creating the perfect home and hosting picture-perfect holiday celebrations straight out of a magazine.

- **Lot Traits:** Homey, Fast Internet
- **Aspiration:** Big Happy Family
- **Personality Traits:** Neat, Perfectionist, Cheerful
- **Likes/Dislikes:** Likes vintage décor, cooking, and baking. Dislikes messiness.

Bucket List:

1. Decorate your home in a 1950s retro style.
2. Max the Baking and Parenting skills.
3. Create a picture-perfect Winterfest with a grand meal and décor.
4. Knit or sew matching outfits for your family.
5. Host a "Holiday Card" photoshoot with your family.

Generation 7: 1960s – The Free-Spirited Caroler

Story Challenge:
You embrace peace, love, and the power of music to bring people together during the holidays. As a free spirit, you wander the world, spreading joy through song and holiday cheer.

- **Lot Traits:** Natural Light, Great Acoustics
- **Aspiration:** Musical Genius
- **Personality Traits:** Cheerful, Creative, Loves Outdoors
- **Likes/Dislikes:** Likes singing, gardening, and meditation. Dislikes conflict.

Bucket List:

1. Max the Singing skill.
2. Travel to every world and perform holiday carols.
3. Grow a "holiday garden" with winter-themed plants.
4. Host a Winter Solstice gathering in the outdoors.
5. Write and publish a holiday song.

Generation 8: 1970s – The Disco Holiday Star

Story Challenge:
You are the life of the holiday party! With disco balls, funky tunes, and festive outfits, you light up every Winterfest celebration. Your dream is to be the most famous entertainer of your time.

- **Lot Traits:** Party Place, Great Acoustics
- **Aspiration:** World-Famous Celebrity
- **Personality Traits:** Self-Assured, Ambitious, Cheerful
- **Likes/Dislikes:** Likes disco music, bold fashion, and dancing. Dislikes boredom.

Bucket List:

1. Max the Dancing and Acting skills.
2. Throw a disco-themed Winterfest bash.
3. Reach 3-star celebrity status.
4. Record a holiday disco album.
5. Create a "Holiday Walk of Fame" with photos of every family member.

Generation 9: 1980s – The Holiday Entrepreneur

Story Challenge:

You're a go-getter with big ideas! Whether it's selling holiday toys or inventing new traditions, you strive to make Christmas bigger and better than ever.

- **Lot Traits:** Penny Pixies, Home Studio
- **Aspiration:** Fabulously Wealthy
- **Personality Traits:** Ambitious, Materialistic, Genius
- **Likes/Dislikes:** Likes entrepreneurship, holiday décor, and tech. Dislikes slow progress.

Bucket List:

1. Build a successful business selling holiday items.
2. Max the Entrepreneur skill or Logic skill.
3. Create a high-tech holiday light display.
4. Host a "Holiday Business Gala" in a rented venue.
5. Make at least 100,000 simoleons through your ventures.

Generation 10: 1990s – The Modern Christmas Visionary

Story Challenge:

You are tech-savvy and obsessed with creating new ways to celebrate the holidays. From creating virtual holiday cards to designing festive video games, you blend tradition with innovation.

- **Lot Traits:** Fast Internet, Geek Con
- **Aspiration:** Computer Whiz
- **Personality Traits:** Geek, Creative, Cheerful
- **Likes/Dislikes:** Likes video games, gadgets, and social media. Dislikes outdated traditions.

Bucket List:

1. Max the Programming and Video Gaming skills.
2. Create a Winterfest-themed video game or app.
3. Host a "virtual Winterfest" using the Social Media career.
4. Complete the MySims Trophy collection as holiday décor.
5. Design a futuristic holiday light show for your home.

Through Frost and Time:
A Winterfest Generational Tale

In the frosty embrace of a snowy dawn, a young dreamer stood on the edge of an untouched land. The air was crisp, the world quiet, and the only sound was the whisper of the wind carrying the promise of a brighter tomorrow. Armed with nothing but hope and a love for the magic of Winterfest, they vowed to create a legacy that would withstand the tests of time—a family rooted in joy, resilience, and the traditions of the holiday season.

From this humble beginning, the family's story unfolds across the decades. Each generation builds upon the last, bringing their unique talents and aspirations to the table. From the first handmade cabin in the 1900s to the glittering Winterfest empire of the 1990s, the family evolves with the times, finding joy even in adversity. Whether it's growing a holiday tree farm, crafting seasonal treasures, performing festive songs, or inventing futuristic Christmas gadgets, each generation adds a new chapter to the tale.

Through wars, depressions, roaring celebrations, and technological revolutions, one thread remains constant: the spirit of Christmas. It's a story of community, love, and the enduring belief that Winterfest is more than just a day—it's a feeling that connects hearts and souls.

Now, it's your turn to guide this family through the decades. Will your Sims honor the traditions of the past, embrace the innovations of the future, and ensure their legacy sparkles like the lights on a Winterfest tree? The story is yours to tell.

Generation 1: The Snowy Dreamer

Story Challenge:

You start with nothing but a love for the holidays and a dream of building a family legacy centered around Winterfest. Begin your journey on an empty lot with zero simoleons. Your first task is to scrape together enough money to build a small cabin and celebrate your first Winterfest.

- **Aspiration:** Friend of the World
- **Personality Traits:** Cheerful, Loves Outdoors, Ambitious
- **Lot Traits:** Off the Grid, Simple Living
- **Likes/Dislikes:** Likes gardening, fishing, and holiday décor. Dislikes modern appliances.

Rules & Bucket List:

1. Start with zero simoleons.
2. Earn money only by gardening, fishing, or crafting holiday items (no regular jobs).
3. Build a small cabin with holiday decorations.
4. Befriend at least 5 neighbors and invite them to your first Winterfest.
5. Create one holiday tradition to pass down to future generations.

Generation 2: The Festive Builder

Story Challenge:
You've inherited your parent's love for Winterfest but want to take it to the next level. Your goal is to expand the family home into a cozy holiday retreat, all while earning money through creative means.

- **Aspiration:** Mansion Baron
- **Personality Traits:** Creative, Perfectionist, Family-Oriented
- **Lot Traits:** Homey, Natural Light
- **Likes/Dislikes:** Likes painting, crafting, and vintage furniture. Dislikes minimalism.

Rules & Bucket List:

1. Only earn money through Painting or Woodworking.
2. Expand the family home to include at least three bedrooms.
3. Decorate the house with holiday lights and a tree every Winterfest.
4. Host a Winterfest party and gift handmade items to all guests.
5. Build a "Holiday Workshop" room to pass down to the next generation.

Generation 3: The Jolly Entrepreneur

Story Challenge:

The family is growing, but funds are still tight. You dream of running a successful business that spreads holiday cheer. Use your entrepreneurial skills to build a thriving holiday shop.

- **Aspiration:** Fabulously Wealthy
- **Personality Traits:** Self-Assured, Ambitious, Cheerful
- **Lot Traits:** Penny Pixies, Great Acoustics
- **Likes/Dislikes:** Likes holiday crafting, sales, and business décor. Dislikes laziness.

Rules & Bucket List:

1. Open a retail store selling holiday items (crafted or collected).
2. Earn enough money to upgrade the family home with luxury furnishings.
3. Max the Entrepreneur or Charisma skill.
4. Complete the Holiday Cracker collection and display it in your shop.
5. Throw a gold-level Winterfest party at your store.

Generation 4: The Holiday Farmer

Story Challenge:
You're drawn to a simpler life and want to bring the family back to its roots. You dream of running a festive farm with animals and crops that embody the holiday season.

- **Aspiration:** Country Caretaker
- **Personality Traits:** Loves Outdoors, Good, Cheerful
- **Lot Traits:** Simple Living, Great Soil
- **Likes/Dislikes:** Likes farming, baking, and country music. Dislikes city life.

Rules & Bucket List:

1. Move to Henford-on-Bagley and start a farm from scratch.
2. Only earn money through farming, selling produce, and animal products.
3. Host a "Holiday Feast" every Winterfest with homegrown ingredients.
4. Befriend the mayor and other townies.
5. Build a barn with festive lights and décor.

Generation 5: The Festive Performer

Story Challenge:
You inherit the family's holiday spirit but want to express it through art and performance. Your goal is to become a famous Winterfest performer, spreading joy to Sims everywhere.

- **Aspiration:** World-Famous Celebrity
- **Personality Traits:** Creative, Self-Assured, Outgoing
- **Lot Traits:** Great Acoustics, Party Place
- **Likes/Dislikes:** Likes singing, acting, and performing. Dislikes criticism.

Rules & Bucket List:

1. Only earn money through Singing or Acting.
2. Reach at least 3-star celebrity status.
3. Perform holiday songs in public venues during Winterfest.
4. Throw a grand "Holiday Concert" party.
5. Decorate your home with autographed holiday-themed memorabilia.

Generation 6: The Winter Designer

Story Challenge:
You're inspired by the glamour of the holidays and want to turn the family home into a holiday mansion. With an eye for design, you dream of creating the most beautiful Winterfest décor and events.

- **Aspiration:** Mansion Baron
- **Personality Traits:** Perfectionist, Snob, Ambitious
- **Lot Traits:** Home Studio, Natural Light
- **Likes/Dislikes:** Likes designing, high-end décor, and luxury. Dislikes clutter.

Rules & Bucket List:

1. Only earn money through interior design or landscaping jobs (via *Dream Home Decorator* or gardening).
2. Upgrade the family home into a luxurious holiday mansion.
3. Max the Gardening and Handiness skills.
4. Host a gold-level Winterfest Gala.
5. Create a "Holiday Legacy Room" featuring heirlooms from past generations.

Generation 7: The Kindhearted Giver

Story Challenge:
You've inherited wealth, but your heart lies in helping others. You dedicate your life to spreading holiday joy by giving back to the community.

- **Aspiration:** Friend of the World
- **Personality Traits:** Good, Cheerful, Ambitious
- **Lot Traits:** Peace and Quiet, Homey
- **Likes/Dislikes:** Likes volunteering, gift-giving, and simple living. Dislikes greed.

Rules & Bucket List:

1. Volunteer with your family at least once per season.
2. Gift one valuable item to a different Sim every Winterfest.
3. Host a charity event to raise funds for a cause.
4. Befriend at least 15 Sims in need.
5. Pass down a tradition of generosity to the next generation.

Generation 8: The Arctic Explorer

Story Challenge:
You're drawn to adventure and want to bring holiday cheer to every corner of the world. From snowy peaks to sunny beaches, your mission is to spread the spirit of Winterfest globally.

- **Aspiration:** Outdoor Enthusiast
- **Personality Traits:** Loves Outdoors, Active, Cheerful
- **Lot Traits:** Natural Beauty, Private Dwelling
- **Likes/Dislikes:** Likes travel, photography, and snow sports. Dislikes being idle.

Rules & Bucket List:

1. Only earn money through travel photography and writing.
2. Visit every world and document its holiday traditions.
3. Build an outdoor retreat with holiday lights and a firepit.
4. Participate in and win the Festival of Snow.
5. Host a Winterfest celebration in a different world each year.

Generation 9: The Jolly Inventor

Story Challenge:
You're the family genius and dream of revolutionizing holiday traditions through innovative inventions and ideas. Your goal is to create gadgets that make Winterfest magical.

- **Aspiration:** Nerd Brain
- **Personality Traits:** Genius, Creative, Cheerful
- **Lot Traits:** Science Lair, Convivial
- **Likes/Dislikes:** Likes robotics, technology, and puzzles. Dislikes routine.

Rules & Bucket List:

1. Max the Robotics and Logic skills.
2. Build a robot that helps decorate for Winterfest.
3. Create at least three unique holiday-themed inventions.
4. Host a "Holiday Science Fair" with your family.
5. Pass down a special invention as a family heirloom.

Generation 10: The Christmas Mogul

Story Challenge:
The family has risen to wealth and influence, and you're determined to leave a lasting legacy. Your mission is to create the ultimate Winterfest empire, ensuring the family is remembered for generations.

- **Aspiration:** Successful Lineage
- **Personality Traits:** Ambitious, Cheerful, Family-Oriented
- **Lot Traits:** Fast Internet, Penny Pixies
- **Likes/Dislikes:** Likes luxury, family gatherings, and tradition. Dislikes conflict.

Rules & Bucket List:

1. Build a multi-million simoleon estate.
2. Host a "Winterfest Legacy Reunion" with all living relatives.
3. Pass down one heirloom or tradition from each generation.
4. Max two skills that reflect your character (e.g., Charisma, Baking).
5. Write and publish a book chronicling the family's rise from rags to riches.

Snowfall Beginnings:
Building a Winterfest Legacy

The crisp morning air carried the promise of a new beginning as snow crunched beneath their boots. The land before them, a vast, empty expanse of Newcrest, seemed lifeless, yet it stirred something deep within. This place, though barren, would soon echo with laughter, sparkle with lights, and overflow with the warmth of Winterfest cheer. But that dream felt distant as they stood in the chill, their only possessions a small sack of supplies and an unshakable resolve.

With no infrastructure, no neighbors, and no certainty of what the future held, they began their journey. Days were spent clearing the land and foraging for essentials, while nights were illuminated by a small fire under the stars. Gardening became their lifeline, as they nurtured each seedling with care, dreaming of a time when the barren lot would transform into a flourishing holiday haven. Every fish caught in the nearby stream and every handcrafted decoration brought them one step closer to that dream.

But they knew Winterfest wasn't just about the decorations or the feast—it was about community. Despite the isolation, they reached out to travelers and wandering Sims, offering warm smiles and inviting them to share stories around their humble fire. Slowly, connections formed, and the dream of a town began to take shape.

As Winterfest approached, the once-empty lot now stood proud with a small, rustic cabin adorned with handmade garlands and a fledgling holiday tree. The first Winterfest dinner, though modest, was shared with five new friends, each carrying their own tales of hardship and hope. Together, they sang carols by the fire, proving that even the smallest spark of holiday magic could light up the coldest night.

This was the beginning of a legacy—a promise to build a town where the spirit of Winterfest thrived in every heart and every home. And as the snow fell gently that evening, the Christmas Settler vowed to pass down this tradition, ensuring the holiday magic endured for generations to come.

Generation 1: The Christmas Settler

Story Challenge:
You're the founder of your family's legacy and the first resident of Newcrest. With no infrastructure, you must build a cozy home and establish the foundation of a festive community.

- **Aspiration:** Friend of the World
- **Personality Traits:** Ambitious, Cheerful, Loves Outdoors
- **Lot Traits:** Off the Grid, Simple Living
- **Lot Challenges:** Creepy Crawlies, Wild Foxes

Bucket List:

1. Start with zero simoleons and build a small cabin using only earned funds.
2. Max the Gardening skill and grow a perfect-quality holiday tree.
3. Befriend five Sims in the area to encourage others to settle in Newcrest.
4. Decorate your home with handmade holiday items.
5. Create and pass down a family holiday tradition (e.g., baking cookies or gift-giving).

Area to Build:
The family's first holiday-themed home with a garden and handmade decorations.

Generation 2: The Festive Farmer

Story Challenge:
Inspired by your family's roots, you decide to build Newcrest's first farm, providing fresh produce and holiday treats for the growing community.

- **Aspiration:** Freelance Botanist
- **Personality Traits:** Loves Outdoors, Family-Oriented, Good
- **Lot Traits:** Great Soil, Natural Well
- **Lot Challenges:** Simple Living, Filthy

Bucket List:

1. Build a working farm with a greenhouse, crops, and chickens.
2. Max the Gardening and Cooking skills.
3. Sell holiday-themed baked goods or produce at a market.
4. Host a "Harvest Feast" Winterfest event using only homegrown ingredients.
5. Create and pass down a secret family recipe.

Area to Build:
A festive farmstead with crops, animals, and cozy holiday decorations.

Generation 3: The Holiday Chef

Story Challenge:
With the farm thriving, you dream of running Newcrest's first restaurant. Your vision is a cozy holiday-themed café that becomes the town's Winterfest gathering spot.

- **Aspiration:** Master Chef
- **Personality Traits:** Foodie, Creative, Outgoing
- **Lot Traits:** Homey, Chef's Kitchen
- **Lot Challenges:** Gremlins, Filthy

Bucket List:

1. Build and run a successful 4-star holiday café or restaurant.
2. Max the Cooking and Gourmet Cooking skills.
3. Serve a signature holiday dish every Winterfest.
4. Host a "Cookies and Cocoa" event for the neighborhood.
5. Create a custom holiday drink and pass it down.

Area to Build:
A cozy, festive café or restaurant decorated for Winterfest.

Generation 4: The Christmas Crafter

Story Challenge:
You love making things with your hands and want to provide festive items for the community. Your goal is to establish Newcrest's first crafting shop filled with toys and decorations.

- **Aspiration:** Master Maker
- **Personality Traits:** Creative, Perfectionist, Cheerful
- **Lot Traits:** Convivial, Home Studio
- **Lot Challenges:** Off the Grid, Reduce and Recycle

Bucket List:

1. Build a crafting shop with a workshop and retail area.
2. Max the Fabrication and Handiness skills.
3. Craft and gift toys to at least 10 children.
4. Sell 25 holiday-themed items through your shop.
5. Pass down a handmade heirloom to the next generation.

Area to Build:
A crafting shop with a festive workshop and retail area.

Generation 5: The Festive Performer

Story Challenge:
Music and performance are your passions. You dream of creating a community theater where Sims can gather to enjoy holiday-themed shows and concerts.

- **Aspiration:** Musical Genius
- **Personality Traits:** Outgoing, Self-Assured, Music Lover
- **Lot Traits:** Great Acoustics, Party Place
- **Lot Challenges:** Cursed, Grody

Bucket List:

1. Build a community theater or performance venue.
2. Max the Singing and Acting skills.
3. Write and perform an original Winterfest song.
4. Host a "Holiday Talent Show" at the theater.
5. Create a family holiday songbook to pass down.

Area to Build:
A community theater or performance venue with holiday decorations.

Generation 6: The Holiday Healer

Story Challenge:

With Newcrest growing, you decide to focus on health and wellness. You dream of building a spa where Sims can relax and rejuvenate during the hectic holiday season.

- **Aspiration:** Inner Peace
- **Personality Traits:** Good, Cheerful, Neat
- **Lot Traits:** Peace and Quiet, Natural Light
- **Lot Challenges:** Simple Living, Reduce and Recycle

Bucket List:

1. Build a wellness spa with holiday-themed décor.
2. Max the Wellness and Fitness skills.
3. Host a "Winter Solstice Wellness Retreat."
4. Provide free spa services to Sims in need during Winterfest.
5. Pass down a family yoga routine or wellness practice.

Area to Build:

A wellness spa with festive holiday touches and calming vibes.

Generation 7: The Mistletoe Matchmaker

Story Challenge:
You believe in the magic of love and want to create a romantic holiday destination in Newcrest. Build a park where Sims can gather and celebrate Winterfest romance.

- **Aspiration:** Soulmate
- **Personality Traits:** Romantic, Outgoing, Cheerful
- **Lot Traits:** Romantic Aura, Natural Beauty
- **Lot Challenges:** Wild Foxes, Creepy Crawlies

Bucket List:

1. Build a romantic park with festive lights and mistletoe.
2. Facilitate at least three successful proposals in the park.
3. Max the Gardening and Charisma skills.
4. Host a "Mistletoe Ball" in the park every Winterfest.
5. Pass down a love story journal to the next generation.

Area to Build:
A romantic park with holiday lights, mistletoe, and cozy seating areas.

Generation 8: The Santa Sim

Story Challenge:
Inspired by Father Winter, you dedicate your life to gift-giving and spreading joy. Build a community center that provides for Sims in need.

- **Aspiration:** Friend of the World
- **Personality Traits:** Cheerful, Generous, Family-Oriented
- **Lot Traits:** Homey, Child's Play
- **Lot Challenges:** Gremlins, Filthy

Bucket List:

1. Build a community center with a gift exchange area.
2. Max the Parenting and Charisma skills.
3. Host a community gift-giving event every Winterfest.
4. Gift handmade or valuable items to 10 Sims.
5. Pass down a Father Winter costume or holiday-themed heirloom.

Area to Build:
A community center with holiday lights, play areas, and gathering spaces.

Emma Spencer

Generation 9: The Frost Guardian

Story Challenge:
As the family historian, you want to preserve the family's holiday legacy. Build a museum celebrating your family's contributions to Newcrest and the holiday spirit.

- **Aspiration:** Successful Lineage
- **Personality Traits:** Brave, Ambitious, Good
- **Lot Traits:** Peace and Quiet, Homey
- **Lot Challenges:** Off the Grid, Cursed

Bucket List:

1. Build a museum showcasing family heirlooms and holiday memorabilia.
2. Max the Handiness and Logic skills.
3. Complete the Holiday Cracker collection for display.
4. Host a family Winterfest reunion at the museum.
5. Pass down a family legacy storybook to the next generation.

Area to Build:
A legacy museum featuring holiday displays and family artifacts.

Generation 10: The Christmas Visionary

Story Challenge:

As the final generation, your mission is to transform Newcrest into a holiday wonderland. Build a town square for Winterfest celebrations, uniting the community in joy.

- **Aspiration:** Party Animal
- **Personality Traits:** Outgoing, Cheerful, Creative
- **Lot Traits:** Festive Aura, Penny Pixies
- **Lot Challenges:** Gremlins, Cursed

Bucket List:

1. Build a grand Winterfest plaza with lights, trees, and a festive market.
2. Host a gold-level Winterfest festival for the entire community.
3. Complete a time capsule featuring heirlooms from every generation.
4. Max the Event Planning and Charisma skills.
5. Pass down the ultimate family holiday tradition.

Area to Build:

A grand Winterfest plaza with holiday markets, lights, and community gathering spaces.

The Spellbound Seasons Challenge

In a world where the magic of Christmas was more than a metaphor, a young Spellcaster named Elara set out on a journey to create a legacy as bright as the stars that lit the Winterfest skies. The air around Newcrest was still, the land untouched and waiting to be transformed. With nothing but her wand, a battered cauldron, and her unshakable determination, she began her quest to build a home where holiday cheer and magic could thrive together.

Elara's days were filled with the hum of spells and the crackle of a potion bubbling over the fire. She conjured light to illuminate her small plot of land and cast charms to ward off the pesky foxes that prowled the woods. Her first earnings came from the potions she sold to wandering Sims—elixirs of warmth to chase away the winter chill and enchanted remedies to heal the heartache of the season.

But magic alone wasn't enough. Elara worked tirelessly, foraging in the woods for berries, growing herbs in her enchanted garden, and fishing by moonlight. Each piece of her small, festive cottage was built by her own hands, enhanced by her spellwork, and decorated with handmade holiday items. Her crowning achievement was a holiday potion she created—The Frosted Elixir—a sparkling concoction that brought joy and calm to all who drank it. She bottled this magic, knowing it would become a treasured heirloom for her descendants.

When Winterfest finally arrived, her home glowed with the warmth of enchantment. She invited travelers and neighbors to join her for a magical feast. The table was laden with food infused with spells of cheer and unity, and the air sparkled with enchanted decorations. As the night wore on, Elara taught her guests the ritual of "Starlight Spells," a tradition she hoped her family would carry forward—a spell cast under the Winterfest tree to protect and bless their loved ones.

As the snow fell softly outside, Elara looked around her small home, filled with laughter and warmth. This was the beginning of a legacy she had only dreamed of, and she knew that the magic of her family and their love for Winterfest would only grow stronger with each passing generation.

Generation 1: The Holiday Spellcaster

Story Challenge:

You've always believed in the magic of Christmas—literally. As a Spellcaster, you're determined to use your powers to create a magical, festive family legacy. You start with little but your wand, your cauldron, and a dream of building a holiday-themed sanctuary for your family.

- **Aspiration:** Spellcraft & Sorcery
- **Personality Traits:** Cheerful, Ambitious, Creative
- **Lot Traits:** Magical Aura, Peace and Quiet
- **Lot Challenges:** Off the Grid, Simple Living

Bucket List:

1. Max the Spellcaster rank and unlock all practical spells.
2. Build a small, festive cottage using only funds earned through magical means (e.g., selling potions or rare finds).
3. Create a unique holiday potion to pass down through the generations.
4. Host a magical Winterfest dinner with enchanted decorations and food.
5. Teach a magical tradition to the next generation.

Area to Build:

A cozy magical cottage surrounded by festive decorations and enchanted gardens.

Generation 2: The Festive Vampire

Story Challenge:
As a vampire, the holiday season is challenging—but you're determined to embrace it! You want to build Newcrest's first gothic holiday-themed mansion and prove that even creatures of the night can spread Christmas cheer.

- **Aspiration:** Master Vampire
- **Personality Traits:** Romantic, Perfectionist, Cheerful
- **Lot Traits:** Dark Ley Line, Private Dwelling
- **Lot Challenges:** Creepy Crawlies, Filthy

Bucket List:

1. Max the Vampire Lore skill and reach Grand Master Vampire rank.
2. Build a grand gothic mansion with holiday décor.
3. Host a Winterfest ball exclusively for vampires.
4. Befriend Father Winter and convince him to attend your vampire ball.
5. Create and pass down a holiday-themed vampire drink recipe.

Area to Build:
A gothic mansion with dark, festive holiday touches and a ballroom.

Generation 3: The Yule Werewolf

Story Challenge:
You're a werewolf who loves the outdoors, even in the snow. You want to build Newcrest's first holiday-themed park and create a space where all Sims—occult or not—can celebrate the season together.

- **Aspiration:** Wildfang Renegade
- **Personality Traits:** Loves Outdoors, Active, Cheerful
- **Lot Traits:** Natural Beauty, Great Soil
- **Lot Challenges:** Simple Living, Wild Foxes

Bucket List:

1. Max the Werewolf rank and unlock all dormant abilities.
2. Build a holiday-themed park with snow activities and cozy seating areas.
3. Host a "Full Moon Winterfest" party in the park.
4. Create a unique werewolf howl tradition to pass down.
5. Befriend at least five Sims and introduce them to werewolf life.

Area to Build:
A holiday-themed park with festive lights, a firepit, and winter activities.

Generation 4: The Jolly Mermaid

Story Challenge:

As a mermaid, you adore the holiday season but feel drawn to the water. Your goal is to build a festive winter beach retreat where the magic of the ocean meets holiday cheer.

- **Aspiration:** Friend of the Ocean
- **Personality Traits:** Good, Cheerful, Loves Outdoors
- **Lot Traits:** Island Spirits, Private Dwelling
- **Lot Challenges:** Grody, Cursed

Bucket List:

1. Max the Singing skill to create a festive holiday carol tradition.
2. Build a beach retreat with a mix of tropical and holiday-themed décor.
3. Host a Winterfest party on the beach with seafood and festive drinks.
4. Befriend at least five Sims and invite them to a festive ocean ritual.
5. Pass down a unique holiday carol inspired by the ocean.

Area to Build:

A beach retreat with festive holiday decorations and a tropical twist.

Generation 5: The Festive Ghost Whisperer

Story Challenge:
You're fascinated by the supernatural and want to bridge the gap between the living and the departed during the holidays. Your goal is to create Newcrest's first haunted holiday museum.

- **Aspiration:** Paranormal Investigator
- **Personality Traits:** Gloomy, Good, Creative
- **Lot Traits:** Haunted, Peace and Quiet
- **Lot Challenges:** Cursed, Creepy Crawlies

Bucket List:

1. Max the Medium skill and unlock the ability to host séances.
2. Build a haunted museum filled with holiday memorabilia.
3. Befriend at least three ghosts and invite them to a Winterfest dinner.
4. Host a séance to summon holiday spirits and uncover family secrets.
5. Pass down a unique ghostly heirloom to the next generation.

Area to Build:
A haunted museum with holiday décor and paranormal exhibits.

Generation 6: The Holiday Alien

Story Challenge:

You're an alien fascinated by human holiday traditions. Your mission is to build a futuristic holiday plaza in Newcrest that blends alien technology with festive cheer.

- **Aspiration:** Nerd Brain
- **Personality Traits:** Genius, Outgoing, Cheerful
- **Lot Traits:** Convivial, Science Lair
- **Lot Challenges:** Gremlins, Wild Foxes

Bucket List:

1. Max the Rocket Science and Logic skills.
2. Build a futuristic holiday plaza with glowing lights and advanced tech.
3. Host an intergalactic Winterfest party, inviting aliens and humans.
4. Collect and display holiday-themed space rocks and alien artifacts.
5. Pass down an alien-inspired holiday tradition.

Area to Build:

A futuristic holiday plaza with glowing lights and alien-inspired décor.

Generation 7: The Winter Sprite

Story Challenge:

You're a mischievous yet kind-hearted sprite who loves to spread holiday cheer. Your goal is to create a magical forest retreat where Sims can escape and celebrate the season.

- **Aspiration:** Nature Walker
- **Personality Traits:** Cheerful, Creative, Outgoing
- **Lot Traits:** Natural Beauty, Peace and Quiet
- **Lot Challenges:** Simple Living, Wild Foxes

Bucket List:

1. Max the Gardening and Handiness skills.
2. Build a forest retreat with magical holiday decorations.
3. Host a forest Winterfest festival with traditional food and activities.
4. Befriend at least five animals in the forest.
5. Pass down a special holiday recipe inspired by the forest.

Area to Build:

A magical forest retreat with glowing lights, festive trees, and cozy firepits.

Generation 8: The Cheerful Skeleton

Story Challenge:

As a skeleton, you're a symbol of life after death, and you love to celebrate the holidays in your own unique way. Your goal is to create a festive graveyard where the living and dead can come together.

- **Aspiration:** Successful Lineage
- **Personality Traits:** Cheerful, Family-Oriented, Brave
- **Lot Traits:** Haunted, Peace and Quiet
- **Lot Challenges:** Grody, Cursed

Bucket List:

1. Build a graveyard with festive holiday decorations.
2. Host a holiday remembrance ceremony for the departed.
3. Befriend at least five ghosts in the graveyard.
4. Max the Medium and Logic skills.
5. Pass down a unique family tradition of remembrance.

Area to Build:

A festive graveyard with glowing lights, holiday wreaths, and remembrance altars.

Generation 9: The Festive Spirit Guide

Story Challenge:

You're deeply connected to the spiritual realm and want to create a sanctuary for meditation, healing, and holiday peace. Build a spiritual center in Newcrest that embraces the magic of the season.

- **Aspiration:** Inner Peace
- **Personality Traits:** Good, Cheerful, Neat
- **Lot Traits:** Peace and Quiet, Natural Beauty
- **Lot Challenges:** Simple Living, Reduce and Recycle

Bucket List:

1. Max the Wellness and Meditation skills.
2. Build a spiritual center with holiday-inspired décor.
3. Host a "Holiday Healing Retreat" every Winterfest.
4. Guide at least three Sims to achieve Inner Peace.
5. Pass down a holiday meditation practice to the next generation.

Area to Build:

A spiritual center with calming holiday lights and serene decorations.

Generation 10: The Christmas Occultist

Story Challenge:
As the culmination of the family legacy, your mission is to unite all the occult families of Newcrest in a grand Winterfest celebration. Build the ultimate holiday wonderland.

- **Aspiration:** Party Animal
- **Personality Traits:** Outgoing, Cheerful, Creative
- **Lot Traits:** Festive Aura, Convivial
- **Lot Challenges:** Gremlins, Cursed

Bucket List:

1. Build a grand Winterfest plaza that represents all occult types.
2. Host a gold-level Winterfest celebration, inviting Sims of all life states.
3. Max the Charisma and Event Planning skills.
4. Complete a family time capsule with heirlooms from every generation.
5. Pass down the ultimate family holiday tradition to all future generations.

Area to Build:
A holiday wonderland plaza with magical décor and activities for all occults.